30 PRAYERS OF
DIVINE
PROTECTION

SUPERNATURAL DEFENSE AND
BREAKTHROUGH IN TIMES OF CRISIS

KYNAN BRIDGES

WHITAKER
HOUSE

Note: This book is not intended to provide medical or psychological advice or to take the place of medical advice and treatment from your personal physician. Those who are having suicidal thoughts or who have been emotionally, physically, or sexually abused should seek help from a mental health professional or qualified counselor. Neither the publisher nor the author nor the author's ministry takes any responsibility for any possible consequences from any action taken by any person reading or following the information in this book. If readers are taking prescription medications, they should consult with their physicians and not take themselves off prescribed medicines without the proper supervision of a physician. Always consult your physician or other qualified health care professional before undertaking any change in your physical regimen, whether fasting, diet, medications, or exercise.

Unless otherwise indicated, all Scripture quotations are taken from either the King James Version of the Holy Bible or the *King James Version Easy Read Bible*, KJVER®, © 2001, 2007, 2010, 2015 by Whitaker House. Used by permission. All rights reserved. Scripture quotations marked (NIV) are taken from the *Holy Bible, New International Version*®, NIV®, © 1973, 1978, 1984, 2011 by Biblica, Inc.® Used by permission of Zondervan. All rights reserved worldwide. www.zondervan.com. The "NIV" and "New International Version" are trademarks registered in the United States Patent and Trademark Office by Biblica, Inc.® Scripture quotations marked (AMP) are taken from *The Amplified® Bible*, © 2015 by The Lockman Foundation, La Habra, CA. Used by permission. (www.Lockman.org). All rights reserved.

Boldface type in the Scripture quotations indicates the author's emphasis. The forms LORD and GOD (in small capital letters) in Bible quotations represent the Hebrew name for God *Yahweh* (Jehovah), while *Lord* and *God* normally represent the name *Adonai*, in accordance with the Bible version used.

Some definitions of Greek words are taken from the New Testament Greek Lexicon—King James Version, based on Thayer's and Smith's Bible Dictionary, plus others (public domain), www.BibleStudyTools.com. Some definitions of Hebrew words are taken from the Old Testament Hebrew Lexicon—King James Version or New American Standard, which is the Brown, Driver, Briggs, Gesenius Lexicon (public domain), BibleStudyTools.com. Other Greek and Hebrew definitions are taken from the electronic version of *Strong's Exhaustive Concordance of the Bible*, STRONG, (© 1980, 1986, and assigned to World Bible Publishers, Inc. Used by permission. All rights reserved.).

Unless otherwise indicated, all dictionary definitions are taken from *Merriam-Webster.com*, 2015, http://www.merriam-webster.com, or *OxfordDictionairies.com*, Oxford University Press, © 2015, 2018 (some spellings have been changed to American usage).

30 PRAYERS OF DIVINE PROTECTION:
Supernatural Defense and Breakthrough in Times of Crisis
(Includes bonus section from *God's Everyday Promises* by Whitaker House)

Kynan Bridges Ministries, Inc. • P.O. Box 159 • Ruskin, FL 33575
www.kynanbridges.com
info@kynanbridges.com

ISBN: 978-1-64123-787-1 • eBook ISBN: 978-1-64123-618-8
Printed in the United States of America
© 2020 by Kynan Bridges

Whitaker House • 1030 Hunt Valley Circle • New Kensington, PA 15068
www.whitakerhouse.com

1 2 3 4 5 6 7 8 9 10 11 ⨇ 28 27 26 25 24 23 22 21

Contents

Introduction

There is no denying that we are living in what the Bible calls *"perilous times"* (2 Timothy 3:1). Regardless of our eschatological viewpoints or denominational affiliations, we can all agree that there is darkness in the world today. Although the times may be perilous, the Word of God remains powerful and unchanging. We read in Isaiah, *"Arise, shine; for your light is come, and the glory of the LORD is risen upon you. For, behold, the darkness shall cover the earth, and gross darkness the people: but the LORD shall arise upon you, and His glory shall be seen upon you"* (Isaiah 60:1–2). And we are assured in Psalm 91, *"He that dwells in the secret place of the Most High shall abide under the shadow of the Almighty. I will say of the LORD, He is my refuge and my fortress: my God; in Him will I trust"* (verses 1–2).

The good news is that we do not have to be subject to the dictates of this world system. We do not need to be fearful or anxious of any plague, war, or rumor of war, because we are citizens of an unshakable kingdom. Even though darkness will cover the earth, the light of God's glory will be visible upon His people. We are the people of God! His glory will be seen upon us in this generation.

The question remains, how do we navigate through challenging times? Is it possible for you to live in victory as a Christian when the world around you seems to be in crisis? The answer is yes! In this powerful book, I share thirty revelatory teachings and prayers to enable you and your loved ones to walk in divine protection and victory—no matter what the news media or society around you says about the state of the world. I lead you in petitions and declarations that will thrust you into the realm of the supernatural in a fresh way, including:

+ Prayer for deliverance

+ Prayer for overcoming fear

+ Prayer for financial breakthrough

+ Prayer for freedom from depression

+ Prayer for overcoming stress

+ Prayer for healing

We know that there is an invisible spiritual enemy who seeks to bring harm and devastation to our lives. The Scriptures give us a prescription for how to handle this enemy: *"Submit yourselves therefore to God. Resist the devil, and he will flee from you"* (James 4:7).

I believe that millions of Christians all over the world are not fully aware of their rights in Christ, and some are even less aware of the spiritual tools they have been given to resist the accuser of the brethren. (See Revelation 12:10.) The world says: "Crisis!" "Pandemic!" "Destruction!" But we must boldly proclaim that God's kingdom is advancing and His people are protected!

Prepare to receive spiritual downloads that will empower you to pray over your spheres of influence and release supernatural deliverance, breakthrough, and defense. I believe that not only will you pray more dynamically, but you and your loved ones will also receive physical and spiritual healing in many areas of your life. Curses will be broken, strongholds will crumble, and divine provision will be manifested.

I make this declaration over you and your family:

Father, I declare that Your peace, power, and protection are released over the homes and communities of Your people. I declare that the *shalom* of God permeates the atmosphere. I declare that the rarified air of heaven fills the very rooms Your people dwell in now. Miracles will be professed and experienced. I declare that nothing the enemy has planned for the people of God will be successful but that all You have planned for them will come to pass. In the name of Jesus, amen!

And now, concerning plagues and viruses, join me in making this declaration:

Father, in the name of Jesus, I thank You for the power of Your Word. Psalm 91:10 declares, *"There shall no evil befall you, neither shall any plague come near your dwelling."* I declare that all virus particles that have been arrayed against me are neutralized, in the name of Jesus. My entire household and I are covered by the blood of Jesus. I speak death, destruction, and disintegration against every virus or other pestilent disease. I declare that all my loved ones are under divine protection. I declare that I have supernatural immunity. I declare that the reign of any virus or related disease will come to a swift end. I break the power of fear, worry, and hysteria, and I invoke the peace of God in every area of my life. Today, I walk in divine health and supernatural recovery, in Jesus' name!

1: Divine Healing

Who his own self bare our sins in his own body on the tree, that we, being dead to sins, should live unto righteousness: ***by whose stripes ye were healed***.

(1 Peter 2:24)

Whether you realize it or not, healing is the children's bread. Healing is the divine inheritance of every believer. Contrary to what many people believe, healing is not just something that God will do if it is His will. Healing *belongs* to us! David said, *"I have been young, and now am old; yet have I not seen the righteous forsaken, nor his **seed begging bread**"* (Psalm 37:25). In other words, God as a loving Father will not neglect His children.

Jesus put it this way, *"For every one that asketh receiveth; and he that seeketh findeth; and to him that knocketh it shall be opened. Or what man is there of you, whom if his son ask bread, will he give him a stone? Or if he ask a fish, will he give him a serpent? If ye then, being evil, know how to give good gifts unto your children, how much more shall your Father which is in heaven give good things to them that ask him?"* (Matthew 7:8–11). If natural parents would not do anything to harm their children, then why would we think that putting sickness and disease on His children somehow pleases God? The devil would have us believe that, but he is a clever liar!

Jesus paid a tremendous price for our healing. By His stripes we were healed from every category of sickness, disease, and infirmity, from the common cold to cancer. I don't know about you, but I refuse to "take on" something that Jesus died to "take off" of my life. Jesus instructed His disciples to ask for their daily bread. (See Matthew 6:11.) Healing is the daily bread of the believer, and through the blood of Jesus we have received a never-ending supply of God's miraculous healing power. Whatever illness, ailment, infirmity, or symptom you or your loved ones might be dealing with, you must understand that Jesus addressed it on the cross. You are already healed, completely and totally!

Prayer of Divine Protection

Father, in the name of Jesus, I thank You that, because of Christ's blood, I am completely and totally healed of any and all sicknesses and infirmities. Thank You, Father, that I am healed completely through the atoning work of Jesus Christ on the cross. Every cell in my body must submit to the lordship of Jesus Christ. Every part of my body functions perfectly. Every fiber of my being is under the control and authority of the Word of God. I am healed and whole in the name of Jesus. According to 1 Peter 2:24, the stripes of Jesus have categorically healed me from all disease; therefore, sickness has no more legal right to operate in my life. I serve the enemy notice that the debt of sin and iniquity has been satisfied on the cross. The penalty of my sin has been paid in full, and I no longer have any outstanding debt. I am free to walk in divine health and fulfill my assignment in wholeness and completeness. I command all lying symptoms to cease and desist in the name of Jesus. Cancer, autoimmune disorders, hypertension, diabetes, issues of blood, arthritis, depression, and any other disease; I command you to leave my body in the name of Jesus. I am healed! Amen!

2: Financial Breakthrough

And he commanded the multitude to sit down on the grass, and took the five loaves, and the two fishes, and looking up to heaven, he blessed, and brake, and gave the loaves to his disciples, and the disciples to the multitude.

(Matthew 14:19)

Many years ago, I was in a state of financial lack. It was so bad that there were even times when I didn't know where my next meal was going to come from. Ironically, I loved the Lord and was aware of many Scriptures on financial abundance—at least, so I thought! However, I was taught that prosperity was an ungodly thing. I was under the impression that it wasn't truly the will of God for me to prosper. Then, one day, I read a verse in the Bible that literally transformed my life: *"And God is able to make all grace abound toward you; that ye, **always having all sufficiency in all things**, may abound to every good work"* (2 Corinthians 9:8). In the *Amplified Bible*, it is even more descriptive: *"And God is able to make all grace [every favor and earthly blessing] come in abundance to you, so that you may always [under all circumstances, regardless of the* *need] have complete sufficiency in everything [being completely self-sufficient in Him], and have an abundance for every good work and act of charity."*

This sure didn't look like the kind of life I was experiencing at the time! Simply put, I was in need of a supernatural financial breakthrough in my life. Remember, without revelation there can be no transformation. Even though I read a few Scriptures, I didn't have a revelation of God's will for my finances, and faith can only operate where the will of God is known. God wanted me to walk in financial abundance. He wanted me to experience supernatural multiplication in my life. In the Gospel accounts, Jesus took two fish and five loaves of bread and multiplied them. (See Matthew 14:19.) God has the ability to take the little that we have and use it to feed multitudes as long as we are willing to trust it in His hands. What if I told you that the breakthrough you were looking for was already in your hands? Release the little that is in your hands, and God will release the abundance that is in His!

Prayer of Divine Protection

Father, in the name of Jesus, I thank You for Your miraculous provision in my life. I declare breakthrough in every area of my financial life. Every Jericho wall surrounding my blessings, prosperity, and finances comes down right now in Jesus' name! All contracts, deals, judgments, opportunities, and lands are released to me right now in Jesus' name. No weapon fashioned against me or my resources will prosper, and I take authority over every devouring spirit that has robbed or hindered the blessings of God from flowing into my life. My mind and spirit are receptive to supernatural opportunities, divine ideas, and witty inventions in the name of Jesus. According to Deuteronomy 8:18, I receive power and ability to get wealth so that Your covenant may be established and Your kingdom advanced in the earth. I live in the reality of Your prosperous plan for my life. Today, I declare that my financial breakthrough has come in Jesus' name. Amen!

3: Soul Prosperity

Beloved, I wish above all things that thou mayest prosper and be in health, even as thy soul prospereth.

(3 John 2:2)

When the psalmist prayed for his beloved city of Jerusalem, a city that symbolized the presence of God with the Israelites, he prayed specifically for peace: *"Pray for the peace of Jerusalem"* (Psalm 122:6). Why peace? We might immediately think of peace from conflict or a ceasefire, and that is certainly true. However, the Hebrew word for peace packs more than the English term: *"peace"* in Hebrew is *shalom*, which means wholeness, completeness, and prosperity. *Shalom* is an all-encompassing term for well-being and restoration on every level.

It is God's will that you and I, too, have *shalom*, that we prosper in every area in our lives. The most important form of prosperity is the prosperity that takes place in our soul. This is what the apostle John was alluding to in his third epistle when he writes this wish that his readers will prosper even as their souls prosper. The Greek word used here for "*prosper*" is *euodoō*, which means "to grant a prosperous and expeditious journey, to lead by a direct and easy way." God wants us to have everything that we need in order to do everything that He has called us to do. Imagine a farmer that doesn't possess plowing equipment or a painter without a paintbrush. They wouldn't get much done! In a similar way, we need *shalom* to be able to get anything done!

God doesn't want us to be lacking in any area of our lives, especially our souls. This means that God wants us to have *shalom* in our mind, decisions, and emotions. The more peace we have in our soul, the more we will experience outward success and abundance in our lives. Remember, prosperity is from the inside out and not the outside in! *Shalom* to you in Jesus' name!

Prayer of Divine Protection

Father, in the name of Jesus, I thank You for Your peace and prosperity in every area of my life. Jesus, I know that You are the Prince of Peace; therefore, I declare that Your supernatural peace floods my soul. I command all fear, chaos, confusion, and despair to leave me now. I declare that I am complete and whole in every area of my life. I have been justified by faith through the Lord Jesus Christ; therefore, I have peace with God. I declare that anything that is contrary to peace in my life is neutralized in Jesus' name. I declare that I walk in divine prosperity. I have an abundance of peace, resources, and blessings. There is nothing missing and nothing broken in any area of my life because of Jesus. I am no longer a slave to chaos and confusion. Circumstances no longer determine my level of peace within, because I am prosperous on the inside. I have a victorious and productive mental attitude. All negativity and cynicism must leave my thought life right now. You said You would keep me in perfect peace if my mind was stayed on You; therefore, I declare that I have perfect peace and I walk in biblical prosperity. There is no lack or insufficiency in any area of my life. Your Word declares that You give me richly all things to enjoy, therefore I rejoice in Your goodness and abundant provision in my life. In Jesus' name, amen!

4: Exceeding Abundantly

*Now unto him that is able to do **exceeding abundantly** above all that we ask or think, according to the power that worketh in us, unto him be glory in the church by Christ Jesus throughout all ages, world without end. Amen.*

(Ephesians 3:20–21)

In John 10:10, Jesus said, *"The thief cometh not, but for to steal, and to kill, and to destroy: I am come that they might have life, and that they might have it more abundantly."* This sounds good, but what does the abundant life look like? First of all, let's look at these two interesting words: *"life"* and *"abundantly."* The word *"life"* comes from the Greek word *zōē*, which means "the absolute fullness of life." The word for *"abundantly"* used in this biblical account is the Greek word *perissos*, which means "over and above, more than is necessary, superadded." Simply put, God wants us to enjoy eternal life (supernatural life) over and above, more than necessary, and exceeding normal measure. That sounds really good!

The problem is that most people relegate eternal life to some future experience, when in fact believers are called to enjoy a supernatural life *here* and *now*. You don't have to wait until you die to experience eternal life. God doesn't desire for us to barely get along while we wait for the "sweet by and by."

The question is, how do we enjoy this abundant life? Paul, in his epistle to the Ephesians, wrote, *"Now unto him that is able to do **exceeding abundantly** above all that we ask or think, according to the power that worketh in us."* The phrase *"exceeding abundantly"* is the same term Jesus used to describe the life He came to give us. In other words, God desires for us to live above circumstances, pain, fear, sickness, rejection, and any other limitations presented to us in the natural realm. He wants us to experience an overcoming life, a life of true victory. The key is found in this phrase, *"according to the power that worketh in us."* If we want to enjoy the abundant life, we must place a demand on it by faith according to the power of the Spirit that is working in us. The greater the demand, the greater the supply!

Prayer of Divine Protection

Father, in the name of Jesus Christ, I thank You for Your amazing love toward me. Lord, I realize that it is Your will for me to live the abundant life for which Jesus died to give me. I recognize that the enemy has come to steal, kill, and destroy, but You have come to impart Your eternal life to me, here and now! I don't have to wait to enjoy the benefits of eternity, because You have called me to walk in the supernatural every day. I declare that Your supernatural power is at work inside of me. You are able to do exceeding abundantly in my life through the power of Your Word operating in my inner being. I declare that sickness, poverty, disease, and oppression are broken by the power of the Holy Spirit working in me. I will never live beneath the abundant life that You have provided for me. I am no longer limited by my circumstances or problems, but I operate in the unlimited power of God's Word. I live a victorious life, and there are no forces in heaven or in earth greater than the Holy Spirit living in me. I will never be depressed! I will never be afraid! I will never be bound again! I declare that the same Spirit that raised Jesus from the dead lives in me, and quickens every area of my life in Jesus' name! Amen.

5: Breaking Curses

Christ hath redeemed us from the curse of the law, being made a curse for us: for it is written, Cursed is every one that hangeth on a tree: that the blessing of Abraham might come on the Gentiles through Jesus Christ; that we might receive the promise of the Spirit through faith.

(Galatians 3:13–14)

Sticks and stones may break my bones, but words can never hurt me!" I'm sure, like me, you chanted this little adage on the playground, maybe to prompt self-esteem or bravery. Well, as nice as this phrase is, it couldn't be further from the truth: Words have tremendous power! Words can hurt and they can heal. Words can invoke blessings or they can invoke curses. As a child, I thought that curses were the result of witches brewing toad feet in a cauldron (thanks to Disney cartoons). Little did I know, back then, that curses were much more subtle, and much more destructive. A curse is defined as a solemn utterance intended to invoke a supernatural power to inflict harm or punishment on someone or something. Every time someone speaks evil over another person, they are, in effect, cursing them. This is why the Scriptures command us to *"bless, and curse not"* (Romans 12:14).

In the Old Testament, God said that He would visit the iniquities of the fathers upon the children, to the third and fourth generation. (See Exodus 34:6–7.) This was another dimension of a curse. Iniquitous patterns can be perpetuated through bloodlines (and also as a result of solemn utterances), giving legal permission to demonic spirits to oppress individuals, families, children, and even communities—often for generations. Before we became born again, we lived under a curse. This curse of sin, sickness, poverty, and, ultimately, death affected every area of our lives.

I have good news for you; through Christ, the curse has been broken off of our lives! Christ became a curse for us so that we no longer have to live under the influence of curses; rather, we have been liberated and empowered to walk in the fullness of the blessing! The key to walking in the blessing is coming into agreement with the blessing and falling out of agreement with the curse. Whatever you agree with is what you give legal permission to operate in your life. Whom God blesses, no man can curse.

Prayer of Divine Protection

Father, in the name of Jesus Christ, I take authority over the spirits of darkness, depression, death, and destruction in the name of Jesus. I now invoke my heavenly rights as a citizen of the kingdom of God, and declare that through the shed blood of Jesus, I am healed, whole, and delivered. I decree that all curses and strongholds are broken off my life and the lives of those I love. I take authority over the spirit of death (premature or otherwise) *right now*. I declare that no weapon formed against Your people will prosper. I let loose the love, joy, peace, wholeness, and protection of God *now*! Send your angels to encamp all around me. I declare that the very *power and presence* of God fills my being from the crown of my head to the soles of my feet. I declare that all spiritual leaders and laborers are covered in the blood of Jesus Christ. I command schizophrenia, hypocrisy, double-mindedness, confusion, depression, despair, loneliness, bipolar disorder, and any other mental stronghold or mind-binding spirit to lose its power and to loosen its hold on the people of God right now, in Jesus' name. The joy of the Lord is my strength! From this day forward, I walk in total and complete freedom and victory. In Jesus' name, amen!

6: Breakthroughs Come Suddenly

And suddenly there was a great earthquake, so that the foundations of the prison were shaken: and immediately all the doors were opened, and every one's bands were loosed.

(Acts 16:26)

Are you ready for your "suddenly" breakthrough? In the book of Acts, Paul and Silas were in prison, and the Bible says that as they prayed and sang, *"suddenly there was a great earthquake"* that shook the foundations of the jail, opened the cell doors, and released everyone's shackles. The dictionary defines *suddenly* as "quickly and unexpectedly." Even though Paul and Silas were praying, they did not know that God would deliver them with such power, speed, and magnitude. This is what a "suddenly" is all about.

Suddenly means that no one will be expecting the miracle to take place in the way that it does. Suddenly means that the doors will swing open so fast and wide that it will cause an "earthquake." When suddenly takes place, natural limitations are dissolved, and time is interrupted by eternity. The laws of delay and stagnation are broken.

Are you ready for a suddenly? God is turning your midnight into a suddenly, in Jesus' name! I declare that your "suddenly season" is upon you now! It doesn't matter how long you may have been in bondage or captivity, God is about to show up in your life in a magnanimous way. You are about to see foundations shaken, doors opened, and shackles loosed.

Prayer of Divine Protection

Father, in the name of Jesus, I declare that my suddenly season is here. I declare that doors open miraculously and all chains are broken off my life. The things that were difficult in the past will not be difficult anymore because of the working of Your supernatural power. Walls come down and doors swing open for me, right now! I am a believer in Your Word; therefore, I release my faith for miracles now. I declare that every work of the enemy that has been operating in my life is destroyed by the power of the Holy Spirit. I declare that praise is my weapon, and I use this weapon to push back the enemy. I take authority over every weapon of the enemy fashioned against me, in Jesus' name. Amen! (See Isaiah 54:17.)

7: Willing and Obedient

*If you be willing and obedient, you shall eat the good of
the land.* (Isaiah 1:19)

My seventh-grade teacher, Ms. Green, frequently taught
her class about the value of obedience. One day, she
told us a story of a little girl who was playing out in the
yard while her grandmother was sitting on the porch. The
grandmother suddenly yelled at the little girl, "Stop!" so she
froze in her tracks. Then the grandmother said, "Now, turn
around and walk this way!" The little girl quickly complied
with these instructions, turning around and walking toward
her grandmother until she arrived on the porch. Her grandmother pointed out at the yard and said, "Look!" As the girl
turned and looked, she saw a copperhead snake right near the
place where she had been playing. If she had hesitated to obey
her grandmother for one second, it could have cost her life.

This is a striking illustration of the value of obeying
trusted authority. How much more important is it for us to
obey our heavenly Father? Often, we underestimate the value

of obedience in the kingdom of God, but it is a key factor in experiencing supernatural breakthrough. The Bible says, *"If you be willing and obedient, you shall eat the good of the land."* This is true for every area of our lives. Yes, we are under the grace of God, and He forgives us when we sin, but nothing can replace obedience. As we obey God, we posture ourselves to walk in His highest and best for our lives. On the other hand, if we disobey God, we remove ourselves from the abundant harvest He has for us.

The word *"willing"* in Isaiah 1:19 comes from the Hebrew word *abah*, among whose meanings is "to consent, yield to, accept." Just as the young lady yielded to her grandmother, we must consciously and consistently yield to the Word of God. The word *"obedient"* here comes from the Hebrew word *shama*, which means "to hear, listen to, obey." We must listen to and obey what God instructs us; the sooner we heed what God tells us to do, the sooner we will prosper. The Bible admonishes us to be both hearers and doers of the Word. (See James 1:22.) As we obey God, we will enjoy *"the good of the land."*

Prayer of Divine Protection

Father, in the name of Jesus, Your Word says that if we are willing and obedient, we will eat the good of the land. I declare that I walk in obedience to Your Word. Romans 10:17 says, *"Faith comes by hearing, and hearing by the word of God."* As I hear Your word, I respond in faith and obedience to Your instruction. "Your sheep hear Your voice, and a stranger they will not follow"; I am one of Your sheep; therefore, I hear Your voice clearly, and I will not follow the voice of a stranger. I declare that I enjoy the good of the land in every area of my life. In Jesus' name, amen! (See John 10:1–5.)

8: Speak Those Things

*(As it is written, I have made thee a father of many nations,) before him whom he believed, even God, who quickeneth the dead, and calleth those things which be not **as though they were**.*   (Romans 4:17)

I grew up at the younger end of a large family. With so many older siblings, I quickly learned how to use words to my own advantage—including threatening others when I felt intimidated, being quick to talk back when bullied or criticized, and a plethora of other verbal skills necessary for survival. I thought, back then, that I could manipulate a situation by my words. I've since learned something far more profound, and far more positive: we can *create* a situation by our words. We literally have the ability to speak things, situations, and circumstances into existence.

This spiritual principle has been hijacked by the New Age community, but make no mistake, it is absolutely biblical! For example, have you ever said that you feel a certain way—that you're sick, upset, frustrated, or depressed? What happens when you speak those words? Immediately, the feeling that you articulated takes root in your mind and emotions, and even your physical body. This is a very powerful phenomenon! Scientists have concluded that words affect our behavior in a very tangible way.

What would happen if you and I would learn to speak God's Word over our lives instead of words of doom and gloom? I believe that we would experience a supernatural mega-thrust into our lives. Jesus said in Mark 11:22–23, *"And Jesus answering saith unto them,* **Have faith in God.** *For verily I say unto you, that whosoever shall say unto this mountain, Be thou removed, and be thou cast into the sea; and shall not doubt in his heart, but shall believe that those things which he saith shall come to pass; he shall have whatsoever he saith."* Notice that the Bible never told us to *say* what we *have*, it said that we would *have* what we *say*! When he was promised an heir, Abraham did not consider his own impotence nor the barrenness of Sarah's womb, but he believed he would be the *"father of many nations"* (Genesis 17:4) despite any physical evidence to the contrary. You and I must learn how to call those things that be not as though they were, and thus become imitators of our heavenly Father.

Prayer of Divine Protection

Father, in the name of Jesus, I recognize that You are the most powerful Being in all the universe. Your Word has the ability to create and to give life. Just as You spoke the world into existence through Your living Word, I speak that same Word over every barren area in my life. In the beginning was the Word, and the Word was with God, and the Word was God (see John 1:1); therefore, I declare that Your Word is the final authority in my life. I make the decision by faith to declare Your Word despite what I see, hear, or feel in the natural world. I recognize that real faith is not the ignorance or neglect of circumstances but dominion over them. Your Word is alive, active, and full of supernatural power. I release that supernatural power now by declaring Your Word. I will not die, but live and declare the works of the Lord. (See Psalm 118:17.) My life is productive, fruitful, and blessed in every area. No weapon fashioned against me shall prosper because I am a child of the Most High God and His supernatural grace covers me completely. I am healed, blessed, prospered, and restored in Jesus' name. I can do all things through Christ who gives me strength in Jesus' name. Amen!

9: Prayers of Protection

He that dwelleth in the secret place of the most High shall abide under the shadow of the Almighty. I will say of the LORD, He is my refuge and my fortress: my God; in him will I trust. Surely he shall deliver thee from the snare of the fowler, and from the noisome pestilence.

(Psalm 91:1–3)

I have come to discover firsthand the reality of divine protection. On one of my mission trips to Liberia, I encountered an extremely perilous situation. I was called upon to preach three times a day for six days straight in a small township outside of Monrovia. It was extremely exhausting, but even worse was what I witnessed during the meetings: people everywhere seemed very sick, and some were even vomiting during the service. I later learned that shortly before I arrived, the Ebola virus had broken out in Liberia.

I had already prayed Psalm 91 over my entire trip, and I had intercessors praying prayers of protection for me back in the States. I declared that no evil would befall my dwelling and that I would be delivered from the *"noisome pestilence."* By the grace of God, I didn't get sick in the slightest. A month after I came back from Liberia, there were reports of thousands of people who had been infected and killed by the deadly Ebola virus. This was wretched and dreadful news! Yet I was in awe and rejoicing that there was no negative impact on me. In addition to this, not a single pastor or parishioner in our ministerial fellowship saw a single fatality from the Ebola outbreak. Glory to God! This is what we call "divine protection." Through prayer, we activated God's promise of protection as outlined in Psalm 91.

Not only do I use this powerful prayer when I travel overseas, but I pray this prayer every day. Every time I travel (by car or plane) I declare, "I dwell in the secret place of the Most High God, and I abide under the shadow of the Almighty. I declare divine protection over every aspect of my journey, in Jesus' name! Amen!" Remember, the Scripture says, *"Ask, and ye shall receive"* (John 16:24). How many areas of our lives could use God's divine protection? We don't have to experience calamity, peril, or chaos in our lives. We have the privilege of dwelling under the shadow of His wings. We can pray this prayer of divine protection over our homes, families, children, churches, schools, neighborhoods, and places of employment. We can dwell in the secret place!

Prayer of Divine Protection

Father, in the name of Jesus, I thank You for Your goodness and grace toward me. Thank You, Lord, for Your divine protection over my life. I declare that I dwell in the secret place of the Most High, and I abide under the shadow of the Almighty. Thank You, God, for being my refuge and safety. I declare that I am covered under the shadow of Your wings and my trust is in Your power and might. I am delivered from every snare of the wicked one and any and all pestilence, virus, disease, infection, or outbreak, in Jesus' name. I declare that no evil (in any form) can come near my dwelling or my family, in Jesus' name. Sickness, disease, and infirmity have no place in my life. Lord, I thank You for dispatching Your angels of protection to go before me and keep me in all of Your ways. I am protected from catastrophe, chaos, accidents, calamity, peril, danger, harm, and destruction in the name of Jesus Christ. I will dwell in peace and safety today, and every day, of my life. A thousand shall fall by my side and ten thousand at my right hand, but destruction will not come near me. I am not afraid of any demonic activity or assignment from the devil, because greater is He who lives in me than he that lives in the world. (See 1 John 4:4.) I am surrounded with a host of warring angels that hearken to the voice of God's Word and who are ready to move at my beckoning call. In Jesus' name, amen.

10: Divine Recovery

And David enquired at the LORD, saying, Shall I pursue after this troop? Shall I overtake them? And he answered him, Pursue: for thou shalt surely overtake them, **and without fail recover all.**   (1 Samuel 30:8)

One of the most frustrating things in life, in my opinion, is losing something of value. For example, I am extremely fond of pens. I consider myself an amateur pen collector. On one occasion, I misplaced a pen that was expensive and one of the best in my collection. When I realized that I lost it, I became very upset! I looked everywhere for the pen but after several months of searching, I decided that the pen was permanently lost, and I gave up. Almost a year later, however, I was looking for some documents in the glove compartment of my car, and to my surprise, I found my precious pen. It was in perfect condition! Glory to God!

You may not be a pen collector like me, but there may be other things in your life that you find extremely precious that have been stolen by the enemy of your soul. Maybe it was your peace, your health, your financial security, your family, or a precious relationship. Regardless of what was lost, however, whether big or small, God desires to bring restoration and recovery to your life.

King David of Israel knew all too well the pain of loss. Once, on his return home from attempting to battle his enemy, he found that his city had been pillaged and burned with fire, and, even worse, that the enemy had abducted his family. Instead of giving in to despair, however, David *"encouraged himself in the LORD"* (1 Samuel 30:6), and asked the Lord whether or not he should pursue what was lost. God responded, *"Pursue: for thou shalt surely overtake them, and without fail recover all."* This attitude of confidence of the restoration of all that God has promised to us should be reflected in our everyday life! When I found my precious pen, my frustration was turned into rejoicing. God is about to turn your tears into rejoicing. You will recover all! I declare that whatever was lost, stolen, or abducted is about to be recovered in Jesus' name. The key is seeking the Lord with all of your heart. As you seek Him, you will receive an impartation of grace and courage to pursue. Do not give up! This is your season of divine recovery.

Prayer of Divine Protection

Thank You, Lord Jesus, for being my Deliverer and Restorer. Through the cross, You have purchased my freedom and victory. Your blood has redeemed me from destruction, atoned for my sins, and made me whole. I declare that any and every good thing that You have ordained for my life that the enemy has seemed to steal, sabotage, hinder, or delay is restored with interest. I declare that the cankerworm and devourer (see Malachi 3:11) must release all provisions, contracts, and opportunities that God has given me in the name of Jesus. I declare that *all* losses stop right now! In Jesus' name, amen!

11: No More Fear

*For God hath not given us the **spirit of fear**; but of power, and of love, and of a sound mind.* (2 Timothy 1:7)

Years ago, I was daily tormented by fear. I can remember being afraid to go to sleep at night because of the nightmares and horrifying spiritual attacks I would experience. It was then that I realized that the kingdom of darkness was very real. I discovered that one of Satan's greatest weapons is fear. Why? Because he knows that you and I will not take authority over something we fear. What is fear? Simply put, fear is timidity or cowardice resulting from a wrong belief system. I also like to define fear as false evidence appearing true! We are told in 2 Timothy that God has not given us a spirit of fear. Wow! This tells us that fear is in fact a spirit, and this spirit does not come from God. God doesn't want us to succumb to the lies of the evil one in the form of fear and ignorance.

Fear comes in many forms. Many people are afraid of failure, others are fearful of being alone, and others still are fearful of death. No matter what fear has attempted to attach itself to your life, you must understand that God has not given you a spirit of fear; instead, He has equipped you with power, love, and a sound mind.

Whenever we are operating in fear, we are neutralizing our spiritual power and authority. Beloved, I don't know about you, but I don't like being afraid! One day, while I was being attacked in my sleep by demonic spirits, I screamed the name of Jesus. Suddenly, the oppression lifted! It was then that I realized that the name of Jesus was stronger than the devil. There is no need to fear the enemy. He has no power in your life except that which you give him. Every fear in our lives is the result of a lie we have believed about God, ourselves, or others; however, the moment we accept God's truth, the power of the lie is broken and fear leaves. The Scripture declares, *"And ye shall know the truth, and **the truth shall make you free**"* (John 8:32).

Prayer of Divine Protection

Heavenly Father, I thank You for who You are and all that You have done in my life. Your Word is the final authority in my life, and Your Word says that You have not given me a spirit of fear, but of power and love, and of a sound mind. I declare that I am fearless in Jesus' name. I will not succumb to fear, cowardice, terror, or intimidation. I possess the mind of Christ, and Christ never operated in a victim mentality; therefore, I walk in bold faith and confidence in every area of my life. I am not a victim; I am a victor in Christ! Fear has no place is my thoughts or emotions in the name of Jesus. The Word of God declares, *"So then **faith cometh by hearing**, and hearing by the word of God"* (Romans 10:17). I am a hearer of the Word of God, therefore; I have great faith. Faith is the revelation of God's Word in action; therefore, I am a doer of Your Word and not just a hearer. No weapon formed against me shall prosper, including fear, worry, or dread. I lift up the shield of faith and neutralize every fiery dart of fear and timidity in the name of Jesus. I declare that all irrational thoughts and phobias must leave me now in Jesus' name. I have no fear because the Lord is the strength of my life and my salvation.

12: The Power of Proclamation

And Jesus answering saith unto them, Have faith in God. For verily I say unto you, that whosoever shall say unto this mountain, Be thou removed, and be thou cast into the sea; and shall not doubt in his heart, but shall believe that those things which he saith shall come to pass; he shall have whatsoever he saith.   (Mark 11:22–23)

When God created Adam in the garden of Eden, one of the first assignments He gave Adam was to name the animals. This was no easy task! In the Hebrew context, names were very significant; they denoted purpose, function, and destiny. By naming the animals, Adam was exercising dominion in the garden of Eden. In the same way, you and I must exercise dominion in the world we live in through the words we speak. Adam was just following in the "footsteps" of his Creator and heavenly Father. God named every celestial being in the created universe, even the sun and the moon. In the midst of darkness, God proclaimed, *"Let there be light!"* (Genesis 1:3). By speaking light into the darkness, God was exercising dominion over the darkness. Similarly, we must exercise dominion over every area in our lives by speaking God's Word. This is what I call divine proclamation.

Jesus, in the eleventh chapter of Mark, spoke to the fig tree, and by the next day, it withered and died. Peter was puzzled by this marvelous phenomenon, and Jesus responded by saying, *"Have faith in God!"* This can also be translated, "Have the God kind of faith!" As we looked at before, He went further to say that *"whosoever shall say unto this mountain, Be thou removed, and be thou cast into the sea; and shall not doubt in his heart, but shall believe that those things which he saith shall come to pass; he shall have whatsoever he saith."* The word for *"say"* in this passage comes from the Greek word *legō*, which means "to teach or name." God has called us to name the things in our lives through the proclamation of His Word. Every time we speak, we are shaping the world around us and teaching things their function and purpose in our lives. I bet you never looked at things from that perspective before! What are you naming the circumstances in your life? Whatever name you call them will be their name and identity!

Prayer of Divine Protection

Father, I thank You for who You are and all that You have done in my life. I thank You, heavenly Father, for Your goodness and unmerited favor that surrounds me daily. Just as Adam named the animals in the garden of Eden, thus exercising dominion over his environment, I exercise spiritual dominion over my environment by proclaiming Your unadulterated Word over my life. I declare that I am the righteousness of God in Christ. I have authority over the enemy. I speak to every mountain (in every form and manifestation) and command them to move in the name of Jesus. I declare that despair, defeat, depression, and dejection have no place in my mind or in my life. I am healed, delivered, restored, and made whole by the power of the blood of Jesus. I declare that my children, family members, coworkers, and friends are blessed. I declare that I walk in total-life prosperity. By the grace of God, I reign in life. Situations and circumstances do not take dominion over me, but rather I take dominion over them. Amen!

13: Too Blessed to Be Stressed

And God said unto Balaam, Thou shalt not go with them;
thou shalt not curse the people: for they are blessed.
                                                    (Numbers 22:12)

No matter what sphere of influence or area of vocation you operate in, you have probably encountered some form of stress. In fact, according to the American Institute of Stress, 77 percent of Americans experience physical symptoms related to stress! Is this the will of God for the believer? Many years ago, I heard the expression "Too blessed to be stressed!" Even if it seems a little cheesy, I love this phrase! It reminds me that God has been too good for me to complain or worry about the circumstances of my life.

In the book of Numbers, God told the backslidden prophet Balaam not to curse Israel, because they were a blessed people. The word *"blessed"* here is the Hebrew word *barak*, which means (among other things) to "be blessed, to kneel, or to be adored." It means to "be endowed with divine favor, protection, and prosperity." Look at how powerful this idea of blessing becomes in the New Testament: *"Christ hath redeemed us from the curse of the law, being made a curse for us: for it is written, Cursed is every one that hangeth on a tree: that the blessing of Abraham might come on the Gentiles through Jesus Christ; that we might receive the promise of the Spirit through faith"* (Galatians 3:13–14).

Through Christ, you and I have received the blessing of Abraham. We are no longer under the curse! In other words, we have been empowered to prosper, and we have been endowed with the favor and goodness of God. It doesn't matter what things look like in your life; God says you are blessed. Why, then, are so many believers' lives filled with frustration, stress, and worry? They are simply not aware of the full ramifications of the blessing. As new covenant believers, we have no business operating in worry or frustration. Some might say, "But everyone has to be stressed sometimes!" Says who? Jesus told us to take no thought for our lives. He told us not to worry about anything! We are too blessed to be stressed!

Prayer of Divine Protection

Father, in the name of Jesus, I thank You for who You are and all that You have done. Today, I declare in the name of Jesus Christ that I am stress-free. Worry and anxiety do not have permission to occupy my mind. I cast all of my cares and concerns on Jesus Christ, for He cares for me. (See 1 Peter 5:7.) I am worry-free and stress-free today! Nothing will separate me from the peace and love of God. I dwell in the *shalom* of God in every area of my life; there is nothing missing and nothing broken. I declare that rivers of supernatural peace flood my soul and mind right now. You said that You would keep him in perfect peace whose mind is stayed on You (see Isaiah 26:3); therefore, I declare that I have perfect peace! The peace of God resonates within my inner being. Nothing has the power or ability to disturb my internal atmosphere. Father, I will walk and thrive in the blessing of Abraham, which You have placed upon my life. I am blessed beyond measure, and there is not a demon, witch, warlock, or agent of darkness capable of cursing me, because I am blessed in the name of Jesus. Amen!

14: Deliverance Prayers

*That if thou shalt confess with thy mouth the Lord Jesus,
and shalt believe in thine heart that God hath raised him
from the dead, thou shalt be saved. For with the heart
man believeth unto righteousness; and with the mouth
confession is made unto salvation.* (Romans 10:9–10)

Whether people realize it and want to admit it or not,
Christians need deliverance. I have heard it said on
many occasions that a Christian couldn't have a demon. This
is simply not true, because it is not biblical. Many times in the
New Testament, when it talks about casting out a demon, it
was not referring to someone who was *possessed* by a demon
but to someone who was *oppressed* by a demon. While it is
true that a born-again believer cannot be possessed (that is,
owned or controlled) by a demon, it is very possible for them
to be under demonic oppression.

For example, the gospel of Luke gives an account of a
woman under demonic oppression: *"And, behold, there was a
woman which had a spirit of infirmity eighteen years, and was*

bowed together, and could in no wise lift up herself. And when Jesus saw her, he called her to him, and said unto her, Woman, thou art loosed from thine infirmity. And he laid his hands on her: and immediately she was made straight, and glorified God" (Luke 13:11–13). A spirit of infirmity, which affected her ability to walk upright, was oppressing this woman. Jesus used the expression, *"Thou art loosed,"* which comes from the Greek word *apolyō*, meaning "to set free, to let go, or to dismiss." This woman was delivered from an evil spirit! Most believers don't think of sickness as an unclean spirit, but it can be in many instances. In fact, the word *"saved"* in Romans 10 also means, "delivered" or "set free." We have been delivered, we are being delivered, and we will be delivered. I want to take a moment and lead you in some deliverance prayers that will enable you to experience greater levels of victory and joy in your life.

Prayers of Divine Protection

For Emotional Bondage: Father, in the name of Jesus, I take authority over any and all forms of emotional bondage, confusion, or turmoil in the name of Jesus Christ. I declare that I am free from spirits of calamity and chaos in Jesus' name. The Word of God declares that the peace of God rules my heart and mind through Christ Jesus; therefore, I loose myself from the plans and schemes of the evil one. Amen!

For Fear: The Word of God declares that I have not received a spirit of fear, but of power, love, and soundness of mind; therefore, I declare that any and all fear must leave my soul and my body *right now* in the name of Jesus!

For Perversion and Addictions: Father, I thank You for who You are and all that You have done in my life. I believe that Jesus Christ is Your Son; I believe He suffered on the cross and died, defeating the wicked one in hell. I believe that Jesus Christ was raised from the dead and is now seated at the right hand of God making intercession for me. Today, I give You, Jesus, complete control of my life. I ask that You forgive me of any and all sin, and that You cleanse me from all unrighteousness. I repent of all sins, known and unknown. I declare that Jesus Christ is my Lord and Savior. I expose my entire spirit, soul, and body to the blood of Jesus Christ, the Word of God, and the fire of the Holy Spirit, and I command anything in me that was not planted by the Lord Jesus to be uprooted in Jesus' name.

For Sickness: Thank You, Lord, for the blood of Jesus Christ which cleanses me of all sin and restores me to a position of righteousness in You. In 1 Peter 2:24 it says, *"Who his own self bare our sins in his own body on the tree, that we, being dead to sins, should live unto righteousness: by whose stripes ye were healed."* Therefore, I declare that I was completely healed two thousand years ago, and sickness no longer has a legal right to operate in my body. The law of the Spirit of Life in Christ Jesus has made me free from the law of sin and death; therefore, I declare that sickness cannot reign in my mortal body. My body is the temple of the Holy Spirit, and I drive out all sickness, disease, and infirmity. I am totally and completely healed! Amen!

15: The Spirit of Python

And it came to pass, as we went to prayer, a certain damsel possessed with a spirit of divination met us, which brought her masters much gain by soothsaying...And this did she many days. But Paul, being grieved, turned and said to the spirit, I command thee in the name of Jesus Christ to come out of her. And he came out the same hour.

(Acts 16:16, 18)

These verses present us with a very interesting scenario. Paul and Silas find themselves followed and taunted by a woman possessed with a spirit of divination. After several days, Paul finally became fed up with her taunting and mockery, and cast the demon out of her. Praise the Lord! The irony is that this woman was speaking things concerning Paul that were true, but she was speaking them in the wrong spirit. In fact, the Bible makes specific reference to the spirit of divination. What was this? The word *"divination"* here literally means "python," referring to Apollo, also called "Pythius," a false god who held much sway over the Grecian beliefs. But think about the imagery here. A python is a large, heavy-bodied, nonvenomous constrictor snake that kills its prey by wrapping itself around and around them until they're strangled. The spirit in this woman (or upon this woman) was a python spirit. Just as the name signifies, the python spirit attempts to choke the life out of believers by oppressing their body, mind, emotions, and spiritual life. Chronic sickness, fear, addictions, and emotional turmoil are just a few manifestations of this evil spirit.

The Bible says that Paul was *"grieved"* by this spirit. The word "grieved" comes from the Greek word *diaponeomai*, which means "to be troubled, displeased, offended, pained, to be worked up." In short, Paul became tired of this spirit! If you and I are going to walk in total freedom from the spirit of python, we have to come to a place in our heart and mind where enough is enough! It is not the will of God for believers to live under oppression and bondage. If you or a loved one are being tormented by a spirit of python, simply do what Paul did and say, "I command thee in the name of Jesus Christ to leave." Take authority over the enemy! Satan has no right to mock, frustrate, torment, or oppress you or anyone you love.

Prayer of Divine Protection

Heavenly Father, I thank You for breaking the power of the spirit of python over my life and the lives of those I love. Your Word declares that You have given me authority over all the power of the enemy and that nothing shall by any means hurt me. Right now, in Jesus' name, I declare that I am completely free from any and all addictions, perversions, compulsions, oppressions, fears, and life-controlling issues. I loose myself (and those I love) from the demonic stranglehold of the spirit of python and command all depression, anxiety, fear, and chronic sickness to leave my spirit, soul, and body right now in Jesus' name! Devil, I loose myself from you and I command you to leave me now! He whom the Son shall make free is free indeed; therefore, I declare my complete and total freedom from this day forward in Jesus' name. I no longer have to live under the grief and distress of a spirit of oppression. I declare that all my loved ones, friends, and coworkers are also delivered from the demonic influence of this evil spirit. In the name of Jesus Christ of Nazareth, I declare the spirit of python broken off my life once and for all. Amen!

16: The Blood of the Lamb

Forasmuch as ye know that ye were not redeemed with corruptible things, as silver and gold, from your vain conversation received by tradition from your fathers; but with the precious blood of Christ, as of a lamb without blemish and without spot: who verily was foreordained before the foundation of the world, but was manifest in these last times for you. (1 Peter 1:18–20)

One of the most significant holy days in the Old Testament was Yom Kippur, or the Day of Atonement. During this sacred time, the High Priest would take a scapegoat and lay his hands on it, symbolically transferring the sins of the entire nation of Israel onto the animal. Then the High Priest would banish the goat into the wilderness, representing the putting away of Israel's sin before God. After that, a spotless lamb would be sacrificed, representing the atoning (expiating) of Israel's sin, and thus cleansing the entire nation of their iniquities. To this very day, Yom Kippur is the most holy day in Israel.

However, Yom Kippur was just a type and shadow of something much more powerful. Two thousand years ago, Jesus Christ became both the Scapegoat and the sacrificial Lamb, sacrificing Himself of the cross of Calvary for the sins of the entire world (not just the nation of Israel), so that all who believe in Him may be redeemed from the curse of sin, and stand clean, forgiven, and justified before a holy God. What a wonderful display of God's goodness! The blood of Jesus Christ has cleansed every born-again believer from their sins, and has transformed us into new creations.

When I was growing up, my mother would use bleach to remove heavy stains from clothing. Depending on how soiled the clothing was, there would sometimes still be a remnant of the original stain. In contrast, the blood of Jesus Christ removes any and all stains and leaves no trace of our iniquities, but washes us completely clean. Hallelujah! The blood of Jesus Christ is more powerful than anything you have ever imagined. It was the only ransom worthy of redeeming us. No matter what you are dealing with in your life, you must recognize that the blood of Jesus Christ is more than able to redeem, heal, deliver, and cleanse you. There is power in the blood!

Prayer of Divine Protection

Father, in the name of Jesus Christ, I thank You for the blood of Jesus. Through your shed blood, I have been redeemed from the curse of the law of sin and death. According to Galatians 3:13–14, You became a curse for me and hung on the tree so that I might receive the blessing of Abraham. Thank You, Jesus, for fulfilling Yom Kippur on my behalf. The Word of God declares that the life is in the blood. You exchanged Your life for mine and paid my ransom. I receive the blood sacrifice that You made for me, and I know that though You I am completely clean and justified. I declare that the blood of Jesus Christ neutralizes every curse. I declare that the blood of Jesus Christ is the title deed for my healing, deliverance, and breakthrough. I serve notice to the kingdom of darkness that the blood of Jesus is against it! The enemy can no longer condemn, accuse, or slander my name because my sins are under the blood of Jesus. Thank You, Lord, for Your mighty power working in and through my life. Just as the blood of bulls and goats had power under the old covenant to atone and bring restoration, so Your blood, as the ultimate payment, has the power to completely restore my total self. The blood of Jesus covers me in every area of my life. Amen!

17: Freedom from Depression

To appoint unto them that mourn in Zion, to give unto them beauty for ashes, the oil of joy for mourning, the garment of praise for the spirit of heaviness; that they might be called trees of righteousness, the planting of the LORD, *that he might be glorified.*   (Isaiah 61:3)

I can remember getting born again in the late 1990s. I can also remember battling with thoughts of depression and despair. There were even times during that season when I contemplated suicide. Who would've thought a young man from a good family and Christian background would entertain such demonic thoughts? The truth is that there are millions of believers all over the world who battle with depression, despair, and despondency. If you do, it does not mean that you are not good enough or not strong enough. It *does* mean that the devil is eager to trap you in a prison of despair. But the good news is that there is lasting freedom in Jesus Christ. In fact, there is no place for depression in the life of a believer. We've been given the *"garment of praise for the spirit of heaviness."* Jesus said that He came to set the oppressed free and to bind up the brokenhearted. (See Luke 4:18.)

Depression is in fact a demonic spirit, but the power of God set me free from the spirit of depression. This is why I have been on a crusade for the last several years of my life to see millions of believers delivered from the insidious nature of this spirit. Freedom is actually much simpler than people realize! The Bible says, if we will confess with our mouths and believe in our hearts that Jesus is Lord and that God raised Him from the dead, we shall be saved. (See Romans 10:9.) That word *"saved"* there also means "delivered." In other words, you and I must realize that Jesus is more powerful than depression, He is more powerful than despair, and He is way more powerful than any form of oppression that the enemy can bring our way. The moment we believe this spiritual truth is the moment that the power of depression is *broken.*

Prayer of Divine Protection

Father, in the name of Jesus, I declare that the spirit of oppression is broken off of my life completely and permanently. I declare that I no longer wear the garment of despair or the spirit of heaviness, but I have received the garment of praise instead. I declare that my future becomes brighter and brighter as I gaze into Your holy Word. I declare that the spirits of despair, hopelessness, rejection, anxiety, and fear are gone from my life. I recognize that Jesus is the Lord of my life. I also recognize that my body is the temple of the Holy Spirit, and there is no place in my thoughts, in my will, or in my emotions for any form of depression, in Jesus' name. I declare that the power of every lie of the evil one is broken off of my life right now. I will never be depressed again! I will never be bound by despair! I walk in total freedom and victory over every form of demonic oppression that the enemy would try to bring to my life. I declare these things in the matchless name of Jesus Christ. Amen!

18: Take Authority over the Spirit of Fear

For God has not given us the spirit of fear; but of power, and of love, and of a sound mind. (2 Timothy 1:7)

The Bible is very clear that God has not given us a spirit of fear, but rather of power, love, and a sound mind. Notice that the writer of 2 Timothy referred to fear as a *"spirit."* Moreover, the Greek word translated *"fear"* in the above verse means "timidity," "fearfulness," or "cowardice." God has not called you and me to be timid or fearful—He has called us to be bold! The Bible actually says, *"The righteous are bold as a lion"* (Proverbs 28:1).

What are you afraid of today? What is the enemy using to intimidate you? Whatever it is, it is time to take authority over it. In other words, God wants you to take courage. Courage is not always the absence of fear; it is often the willingness to move forward *in the face of fear.* When we are courageous, we are telling fear, "You have no power over me!" Whether it's a negative report from the doctor, a failed marriage, unruly children, or anything else, God is more than able to bring you through it. Do not be afraid; God is with you! It is time for you to stand on His Word and watch Him bring you into the manifestation of what He has promised for your life.

Prayer of Divine Protection

Father, Your Word declares that You have not given me a spirit of fear, but of power, love, and a sound mind. Therefore, I declare that no weapon formed against me will prosper. I refuse to cower in the face of fear, and I refuse to be manipulated by my emotions. I will not allow what I see to control my life. I am not moved by what I see. I am not moved by what I hear. I am moved only by the Word of God. I declare that I have faith and confidence in God's Word. In Jesus' name, amen! (See Isaiah 54:17.)

19: Elisha's Prayer

And Elisha prayed, and said, LORD, I pray You, open his eyes, that he may see. And the LORD opened the eyes of the young man; and he saw: and, behold, the mountain was full of horses and chariots of fire round about Elisha.

(2 Kings 6:17)

Gehazi, the servant of the prophet Elisha, woke up one morning and saw the city surrounded by horses and chariots. The king of Syria had sent soldiers to bring Elisha to him, because he'd found out the prophet had been revealing his secret plans to the king of Israel. Panicked, Gehazi asked Elisha, in effect, "What are we going to do?" Elisha responded, *"Fear not: for they that be with us are more than they that be with them."* (See 2 Kings 6:15–16.)

Have you ever felt like you were surrounded by enemies? Have you looked around and noticed that worry, fear, insecurity, or chaotic family issues seemed to be closing in on you on every side? Have you ever woken up and said to God in a panic, "Lord, what are we going to do? What are *You* going to do?" You may have felt that way last year, last month, or even just this morning. Many times, we tend to get carried away by what we see in the natural and completely disregard what is happening in the spiritual realm. But we can trust that God is active in our lives, no matter what the circumstances look like. The Lord Jesus says that the heavenly Father is always working. (See John 5:17 NIV.)

Elisha prayed that his servant's eyes would be opened to see the activity happening beyond his natural sight, and Gehazi immediately saw numerous fiery chariots and horses on the mountain. God had sent an army to support them! Accordingly, every time a problem arises, allow your spiritual eyes to see beyond your natural understanding. The solution to any problem is always available to us; we gain access to it through prayer and belief in the promises of God's Word. God has already supplied what you need for any present or future situation. Remember this, speak it, and thank Him for it! I declare to you the words Elisha spoke to his servant: "Do not fear—there are more with you than there are with them!" With God on your side, you are the majority! Beloved, don't you believe He will do the same for you as He did for Elisha if you will only ask? Believe and declare what God has spoken, and you will see that the armies of heaven are at your disposal, ready to do battle on your behalf!

Prayer of Divine Protection

Father, Your Word tells me that You are always with me, and that if God is for me, who can be against me? Weapons may be formed against me, but they cannot prosper in my life, in Jesus' name! I do not fear, because You are on my side. You show me strategies and give me instructions to solve any problem. I trust You completely, and when enemies of my faith like worry, despair, fear, and confusion attempt to surround me, I look up and see Your provision and protection encircling me on every side. I declare that no enemy of my faith has power over me, because greater is He who lives within me than he who is in the world! I will keep my spiritual eyes open so that I don't miss a moment of the glorious things You are doing in my life and in the lives of those around me. You are the God who defends me; You are my Banner of Victory. I can't lose, because You are with me. In Jesus' name, amen! (See Psalm 139:7–10; Matthew 28:20; Romans 8:31; Isaiah 54:17; Psalm 118:6; John 4:4; Exodus 17:15–16 NIV.)

20: Faith Is...

Now faith is the substance of things hoped for, the evidence of things not seen.   (Hebrews 11:1)

There is nothing more vital to the Christian experience than faith. Many people would cite prayer, intimacy with God, or love as being supreme—but each of these is connected to our faith in God. The Bible says, *"He that comes to God must believe that He is, and that He is a rewarder of them that diligently seek Him"* (Hebrews 11:6). The foundation of our faith is the confidence that God is who He says He is. The more we operate in the revealed knowledge of God, the more we will experience breakthrough and victory in our lives.

You may be experiencing a difficulty in your life right now. Let me reassure you that God is the Deliverer. God is the Provider. God is the Healer. Yet faith sees the nature and character of God, not just the ability of God. We must make a decision not to be manipulated or persuaded by our circumstances, but rather be fully persuaded by our faith in God and His Word. The term *"substance"* in Hebrews 11 comes from the Greek word *hypostasis*, which literally means "a setting under," or "support." In other words, faith is a support system for every area of our spiritual lives. Without faith, we cannot please God! (See Hebrews 11:6.) But through faith, not only are we able to please God, but we are also able to confidently receive the things He has freely given to us. So beloved, do not be moved by what you see, but stand on the Word of God. Whatever He has promised, He is faithful to perform. (See, for example, Hebrews 10:23.) Faith is the revelation of God's Word in action; therefore, believe His Word and confidently act upon what He has spoken.

Prayer of Divine Protection

Father, Your Word is true! *"Faith is the substance of things hoped for, the evidence of things not seen"*; therefore, I declare that I possess unwavering faith in Your Word. My faith is the evidence that convicts my conscience and serves as the proof that what You have spoken, You are able to perform. I am not moved by my circumstances, but I am confident in Your eternal Word. I wait with great anticipation to see and experience the manifestation of Your glorious promises. My faith allows me to access the realm of the invisible and receive supernatural blessings in every area of my life. I possess my healing and my deliverance by faith. Nothing is impossible to me because I am a believer in Your Word and not a doubter. By faith, I release supernatural breakthrough in my life. Thank You in advance for the manifestation of what You have promised. In Jesus' name, amen!

21: The Unseen Realm

Through faith we understand that the worlds were framed by the word of God, so that things which are seen were not made of things which do appear.

(Hebrews 11:3)

Years ago, I heard a story about several young students who participated in a science project. Their teacher had brought them to a lake, where they were asked to take samples of the water. The instructor then asked the students what they saw in the water they had collected. They didn't see anything, because the water was fairly clear. Then they took the water to the school lab, put some of it on a petri dish, and placed it under a microscope. As the students looked in the microscope, to their surprise, they saw that the water was teeming with life. Even though the organisms in the water were unseen to the naked eye, they were very much real. Over the years, numerous biology students worldwide have had a similar experience.

People often think that "unseen" equates to being "unreal," but nothing could be further from the truth. The unseen realm, or spiritual realm, is just as real—if not more real—than our natural world. How many times have you used a cellular phone? Now, how many times have you seen a cellular frequency? We never question the reality and power of our cellular devices, even though we can't see how they operate. Yet millions of people do not know about or acknowledge the spiritual world—with many people denying its existence and reality.

Today, God desires to open your spiritual eyes so you can see the supernatural realities around you. Faith is the microscope—and telescope—of the spiritual realm. That is why the Bible says, *"Through faith we understand that the worlds were framed by the word of God, so that things which are seen were not made of things which do appear."* How would our lives change if we really understood this spiritual truth? God's words created the physical world; in the same way, God's words will change your world. Speak the Word of God and watch the unseen come into manifestation.

Prayer of Divine Protection

Father, I recognize that You are here in the "eternal now," and I also acknowledge that the invisible realm is more real and tangible than the visible realm. Open my spiritual eyes to perceive and understand the supernatural realities of Your kingdom. I declare that my spiritual eyes are open to see angels. I declare that my spiritual ears are receptive to heavenly wisdom. I declare that I am able to recognize Your supernatural solutions. Father, grant me heavenly vision. I declare that I look beyond my circumstances as I hold on to the reality of Your Word. In Jesus' name, amen.

22: Will You Be Made Whole?

When Jesus saw him lie, and knew that he had been now a long time in that case, He says to him, Will you be made whole? (John 5:6)

One of the simplest—but most powerful—realities of the New Testament is that God wants us to be whole. What is wholeness? Wholeness means that nothing is missing and nothing is broken. God wants us to be fully furnished and thoroughly supplied. The man at the Pool of Bethesda, whom we discussed in yesterday's devotional, had a serious problem: he was disconnected from God. His sin and his sickness had alienated him from God's perfect will. As a result, he was waiting for the *"water"* (John 5:7) to move so he could be healed—since an angel would supposedly stir the water and allow those who could make it into the water in time to be made well.

Are you waiting for the "water" to move? That is, are you waiting for God to do something that He has actually already done? Ironically, the lame man was waiting for God to move—but God was waiting for him to move. *"Rise, take up your bed, and walk"* (John 5:8) were Jesus' timeless words to the man. The Greek word translated *"rise"* means "to waken," or "to rouse"—as when you wake someone up who is sleeping. This man was in a "slumbering" state—both spiritually and physically. The next thing Jesus told the man to do was to take up his bed. This phrase refers to an exercise of the will—to deliberately decide to no longer be in the situation that one is in. Notice that Jesus didn't take up the bed for him. The man had to take up his own bed. Lastly, Jesus told him to *"walk."* The original Greek term means, among other things, "to make due use of opportunities."

What opportunity have you missed as a result of your bondage? It is time for you to make a decision that you are no longer going to be bedridden, but you are going to be bound to your God-given destiny. Wholeness is your portion, because Jesus has provided an abundant life for us. Will you receive it?

Prayer of Divine Protection

Father, in the matchless name of Jesus, I hear Your voice today. Your Word declares that "Your sheep hear Your voice, and a stranger they will not follow." I realize that You are inviting me to experience Your abundant life. I refuse to camp by the pool of despair. I refuse to dwell in a ditch of depression. Lord Jesus, You are the living Word, and Your Word is powerful and miraculous. I respond to Your invitation to receive supernatural life. Your Word tells me to *"arise"* and *"shine."* Nothing will keep me from arising and shining. I will no longer rest upon any affliction, pain, sickness, or rejection. I will walk out my destiny with faith and confidence in You. Today is an awesome day because I serve an awesome God! In Jesus' name, amen. (See John 10:1–5; Isaiah 60:1.)

23: Resurrection Power

But if the Spirit of Him that raised up Jesus from the dead dwell in you, He that raised up Christ from the dead shall also quicken your mortal bodies by His Spirit that dwells in you. (Romans 8:11)

The Scripture tells us that the same Spirit who raised Jesus from the dead dwells within us. If you really embraced that truth, how would it change the way you view your life right now? I often hear people make the statement, "I'm only human." This is a socially acceptable statement—but it is not a biblical one. You are not just human. As a born-again believer, you have the same Spirit who resurrected our Lord dwelling within you! The God of all creation lives inside you. The more conscious you are of the Risen One living within you, the more you are able to release His power in your life.

The Holy Spirit is much more than a religious phenomenon—He is a living Person; He is the very Spirit of God and of Jesus Christ. If you could really comprehend who dwells within you, you would never accept a mediocre existence again. I challenge you to change the way you look at yourself. I challenge you to refuse to live in a defeated way. I challenge you to recognize that there is power inside you.

One of the Greek words translated "power" in the New Testament is *dunamis*, which refers to miracle-working power. It is where we get the English word *dynamite*. So, the next time someone asks you how you're doing, I want you to tell them, "I'm dynamite!" The dynamic power of heaven is working on your behalf. All you have to do is believe and release your faith for the miraculous power of God to operate in every area of your life.

Prayer of Divine Protection

Father, in the name of Jesus, I thank You for changing me. I thank You for the life-giving power of restoration that lives inside me. The fullness of the Spirit of Christ lives within me, and I am working in partnership with the dynamic power of heaven. I declare that God's miracle-working power is touching and transforming every area of my life. I no longer walk in defeat but according to the dynamic power of God. I am victorious, in Jesus' name. Amen.

24: Radical Breakthrough

And it came to pass, when she travailed, that the one put out his hand: and the midwife took and bound upon his hand a scarlet thread, saying, This came out first. And it came to pass, as he drew back his hand, that, behold, his brother came out: and she said, How have you broken forth? this breach be upon you: therefore his name was called Pharez. (Genesis 38:28–29)

I will never forget the day my son Isaac was born. As we were waiting for him to come forth, to our surprise, he literally burst out of the womb. In fact, he came so fast that if it weren't for the nurse who caught him by the heels, he would have literally hit the floor. It's appropriate that his name is Isaac, because every time we think about the story, we bust out in laughter.

In the above passage, the midwife who delivered Pharez experienced a similar situation. This baby's brother was set to come out of the womb first. Yet God had other plans, and Pharez became the firstborn. The name *Pharez* essentially means "breakthrough." Two characteristics of breakthrough are *sudden* and *supernatural*. Breakthroughs are not based on our level of education, affluence, or even natural talent; they are the result of the supernatural power of God.

I believe we are living in a season of supernatural breakthrough. In fact, you are about to embark on the greatest time of your life. The midwife asked Pharez, in effect, "How did you break through?" and people are going to ask you the same question when they see the supernatural manifestation of God's promises in your life. They will want to know: "How did your marriage turn around so quickly?" "How were you instantly healed?" "How did your ministry take off?"

My desire is to set you up for a radical breakthrough. And while breakthroughs are sudden, they are far from spontaneous—the key is faith. Don't forget that "*faith is the substance of things hoped for, the evidence of things not seen*" (Hebrews 11:1). Simply believe, and God will confirm His Word to you with signs and wonders. (See Mark 16:20.)

Prayer of Divine Protection

Father, I acknowledge that You are the Lord of the breakthrough. I recognize that Your miraculous hand is in manifestation in my life. Supernatural doors open for me because I am connected to a supernatural God. I declare that I am in a season of release. Today, I will encounter miracles. I will experience the supernatural grace of God. I will testify of the goodness of the Lord in every area of my life. Many will ask me, "How did you break through?" I will answer them by declaring that miracles are my portion. In the mighty name of Jesus, amen.

25: His Power Is Present

And it came to pass on a certain day, as He was teaching, that there were Pharisees and doctors of the law sitting by, which were come out of every town of Galilee, and Judaea, and Jerusalem: and the power of the Lord was present to heal them. (Luke 5:17)

When Jesus walked the earth, He partnered with God's anointing to see miracles manifested. We see an example of this in the situation described above, in which Jesus was teaching, and *"the power of the Lord was present to heal."* I want you to know that the power of the Holy Spirit is present to heal or deliver you from any difficulty you are facing. Yet your ability to receive a miracle is often contingent upon how sensitive you are to the anointing. Once, while I was in the middle of preaching at a particular church, I strongly felt the presence of God, and I began to call people forward for physical healing. The power of God manifested, and many people were healed and delivered. If we are going to live like Jesus, we must be sensitive to the anointing of the Holy Spirit.

You could say that God's power works according to the "law of supply and demand." You must place a claim, or a "demand," upon the anointing. This is what the woman with the flow of blood did when she touched the hem of Jesus' garment. Power went out from Him and into her need, and she was healed. Jesus told her, *"Daughter, be of good comfort: your faith has made you whole; go in peace."* (See Luke 8:43–48.) Begin to ask God to grant you the sensitivity to His Spirit that will allow you to access His power. Whatever the need is, the supply of the Spirit is available to meet it.

Prayer of Divine Protection

Father, in the name of Jesus, I thank You for the anointing of the Holy Spirit. I recognize that Your Spirit is of priceless value. Right now, I release my faith to receive Your supernatural power working in and through my life. Thank You, Father, for the gift of spiritual sensitivity. I believe that Your power is available right now to touch, heal, and deliver me. I receive the dynamic, yoke-destroying, burden-removing power of God and its working right now. My life will never be the same for having been touched by Your anointing. In Jesus' name, amen.

26: Teach Me How to Prosper

*Beloved, I wish above all things that you may prosper
and be in health, even as your soul prospers.*

(3 John 1:2)

Have you ever come to the end of yourself? Have you ever been so desperate that you just cried out to God for answers? Years ago, I was in a desperate place in my relationship with God and in my personal finances. At that time, I didn't have the understanding of God's favor and blessings that I do today. I couldn't pay my bills or provide for my family the way I know I should have. One night, out of frustration, I cried out to God, saying, "Teach me how to prosper." That was one of the first times in my life that I had actually acknowledged I didn't know something. When I made that request, something broke inside of me. All of a sudden, I began to receive revelation directly from God. He showed me it was His perfect will for me to prosper in every area of my life. The truth is, until I received that revelation, I didn't really believe that God wanted me to prosper. "Religious" people had taught me that prosperity was a sin, and I had believed it; therefore, for a long time, I couldn't receive the notion that God desired to bless me.

You may be thinking, *You mean to tell me that God wants me to have more than enough?* Absolutely! The Bible says, "*Beloved, I wish above all things that you may prosper and be in health, even as your soul prospers.*" Simply put, God wants you to be whole in every area of your life. The Greek word for "*prosper*" here essentially means to have sufficient resources for the journey. In other words, to live in prosperity is to have everything you need to do everything God has called you to do. When we look at prosperity from this angle, it is clear that the most selfish thing we can do is *not* prosper!

I believe God wants to radically shift your thinking in the same way He shifted mine years ago. He wants to challenge you today to believe Him for more. God desires you to understand that there is no request you can make of Him that will deplete His resources or intimidate Him. I encourage you to ask the same question of the Lord that I asked: "Teach me how to prosper."

Prayer of Divine Protection

Father, in the name of Jesus, I thank You for Your perfect plan of prosperity for my life. I declare that I prosper and am in health, even as my soul prospers. As a result of this prosperity, I am thoroughly furnished and fully supplied to perform every good work that You ordained for me before the foundation of the world. As the seed of Abraham, I declare that there is no lack in my life. The spirit of poverty is destroyed. I have no need of aid or support, but every earthly blessing operates in my life. I daily function from a place of abundance. I declare that all grace abounds toward me—always and in every situation. *"It is more blessed to give than to receive"*; therefore, I declare I am a giver. I am a lender and not a borrower. I am blessed in the city and blessed in the field. Thank You, Lord Jesus, that through Your power, grace, and love, my life is a storehouse for those who have needs. My life is a wellspring of supernatural resources, and I am a distributor of blessings. In Jesus' name, amen. (See Galatians 3:7–9, 14; 2 Corinthians 9:8; Acts 20:35; Deuteronomy 28:3, 12.)

27: Mind Control

*Casting down imaginations, and every high thing that
exalts itself against the knowledge of God, and bringing
into captivity every thought to the obedience of Christ.*

(2 Corinthians 10:5)

One of the important elements of supernatural living is
the responsibility of taking our thoughts captive *"to the
obedience of Christ."* We must renew our minds according to
the Word of God. Nothing can substitute for the supernatural power of a transformed mind.

The enemy constantly bombards our minds with
thoughts, suggestions, and even arguments that are hostile
to the Word of God. But our minds do not have to be the
playpen of the devil. Neither do they have to be his dump-
ing ground. We have been empowered to take control of
our minds so that our thoughts are aligned with the mind
of Christ. That's right, beloved. God has given you the authority to exercise control over your thought life. The Bible
says, *"(For the weapons of our warfare are not carnal, but mighty*

through God to the pulling down of strongholds;) casting down imaginations, and every high thing that exalts itself against the knowledge of God" (2 Corinthians 10:4–5).

We must learn how to bring our thoughts captive to the obedience of Christ. The best way to get rid of a stronghold is to replace it with another. Thus, we must establish the Word of God as the stronghold in our mind. This is why David declared, *"The name of the LORD is a strong tower: the righteous runs into it, and is safe"* (Proverbs 18:10). Accordingly, the Word of God must be the fortress that we establish in our minds and hearts to evict the thoughts and attitudes of the enemy and erect the thoughts and attitudes of God. Beloved, it is time for you to take control of your mind. No longer allow the reckless thoughts and ideas of the enemy to permeate the atmosphere of your thought life. The Bible tells us that Jesus Himself is the Word of God. (See, for example, John 1:1, 14.) Declare that you have the mind of Christ. The Scripture says, *"You will keep him in perfect peace, whose mind is stayed on You: because he trusts in You"* (Isaiah 26:3). Exercise your spiritual authority today over the thoughts of your mind, and live in victory.

Prayer of Divine Protection

Father, thank You that I have the mind of Christ. I take captive every thought that is hostile to the knowledge of God and bring it into obedience to Christ. I declare that my mind will no longer be the devil's playground. I evict every single thought or suggestion that is demonic or unclean. My mind is holy; therefore, I declare that it is sanctified, in the name of Jesus. Fear, worry, depression, and anxiety have no place there. I declare that my mind is a fortress of purity and righteousness. I command every false and evil thought that has been sent against my mind to be returned to sender. In Jesus' name, amen!

28: Praise Your Way Through

And at midnight Paul and Silas prayed, and sang praises to God: and the prisoners heard them. And suddenly there was a great earthquake, so that the foundations of the prison were shaken: and immediately all the doors were opened, and every one's bands were loosed.

(Acts 16:25–26)

Years ago, I was talking to a mentor of mine, and he challenged me in a way I had never been challenged up to that point. He said to me, "Kynan, stop trying to pray your way into the presence of God, and start praising your way into the presence of God." Honestly, at the time, I didn't understand what he was talking about. But several months later, I began to comprehend what the Lord was trying to tell me. You see, I had focused much of my energy struggling to pray, often with no breakthrough. Have you ever had seasons when your prayer life was dry? That was exactly how I felt until the Lord gave me this revelation. As I began to implement praise in the manner in which my mentor had instructed me, I saw a drastic shift in the way I encountered God's presence. These words resonated in my spirit: "Praise your way through."

Whatever situation you face today, you need to learn to use praise as a weapon of spiritual warfare. Your praise is like the battering ram of the Spirit. Paul and Silas understood this concept very well. When they were trapped in prison with nowhere to go, they employed the power of praise. They praised their way through the captivity. The Bible records that as they praised and sang, the Holy Spirit invaded the room. Their bands were loosed and the prison cells were opened. (See Act 16:12–33.) What if I told you that praise could break you out of any situation that you're in? If we would simply learn to praise our way through—not complaining or worrying but praising the name of the Lord—we would experience breakthrough. Praise is simply recognizing and acknowledging who God is and what He is able to do. We need to thank God for what He has already done in our lives.

God is more than able to deliver you out of any situation you face. If you are battling sickness and disease, praise your way through it. If you are stuck in a rut, praise your way through it. If you are in debt, praise your way through it. No matter what the difficulty, praise is the battering ram that will break you out.

Prayer of Divine Protection

Father, I thank You for who You are and all that You have done in my life. I declare that praise is one of my weapons of spiritual warfare, and I use this weapon to break out of any situation that would hold me in captivity. Just as Paul and Silas prayed and sang praises, and the Holy Spirit broke them out of prison, I declare that as I pray and praise, the power of the Holy Spirit will be released and break all shackles of bondage off my life. My worship is "my warship." I will use the weapon of praise and demolish the strongholds of the enemy, right now, in the name of Jesus. Amen.

29: Divine Strategies
for Breakthrough

And Elisha sent a messenger to him, saying, Go and wash in Jordan seven times, and your flesh shall come again to you, and you shall be clean. (2 Kings 5:10)

Many people come to me seeking God's supernatural intervention in their lives—they want God to do a miracle for them. They are not alone. All of us want God to do for us what we cannot seem to do on our own. We want to see His miraculous hand move on our behalf.

Yet while it is true that God is a God of miracles, He is also practical. What do I mean by that? Throughout Scripture, we see that every time God manifested a miracle on someone's behalf, it was because they had obeyed a divine instruction that involved the natural world. This tells me that God is a God of strategy; thus, at times, He will give us the solutions we need in the form of strategies or procedures. These are specific instructions that, once obeyed, cause miraculous things to happen in our lives.

Such was the case with Naaman. This man had an important position as commander of the Syrian army. However, he had a serious problem—he was a leper. Naaman went to the prophet Elisha in Israel seeking a solution. He knew that this man of God was a miracle worker and that the prophet could grant him access to God's supernatural healing. So, you can imagine his frustration when Elisha told him to bathe in the Jordan River seven times. What? The Jordan River? It was one of the filthiest rivers of the day. Yet this was the strategy God had provided for Naaman in order to receive healing and turn his life around.

God will often tell us to do something so simple that following it seems ineffective, so we delay—as did Naaman. But when Naaman finally obeyed the instruction, his leprosy was cleansed instantly. (See 2 Kings 5:1–14.) Similarly, I believe there is a divine strategy that, once implemented, will supernaturally shift your life. It could be as simple as any of these: "Wake up in the morning and pray." "Call this person." "Write this book." "Go to this conference." Whatever it is, if you will simply say, "Here I am, Lord; send me" (see Isaiah 6:8), your life will change forever. Today, ask God to give you the strategy that you need to break through.

Prayer of Divine Protection

Father, I recognize that You are a God of strategy. You know the end from the beginning. You instruct and teach me in the way that I should go. I position myself right now in obedience to You so that You can place Your "super" on my natural. It is clear that I live in the accelerated manifestation of the blessings of God as I obey Your Word. My spirit is receptive to divine strategies, in Jesus' name. I thank You for revelation knowledge flowing in my spirit. Right now, I receive divine strategies for my business, my ministry, my marriage, and my finances. According to Your Word, no weapon formed against me will be able to prosper. Thank You for downloading divine blueprints for success. In Jesus' name, amen. (See Psalm 32:8; Isaiah 54:17.)

30: Make Room for Your Miracle

And she [the Shunammite woman] said to her husband, Behold now, I perceive that this is a holy man of God, which passes by us continually. Let us make a little chamber, I pray you, on the wall; and let us set for him there a bed, and a table, and a stool, and a candlestick: and it shall be, when he comes to us, that he shall turn in there.

(2 Kings 4:9–10)

Are you prepared for what God desires to do in your life? I know that might seem like a strange question, but it is a very important one. In other words, can you accommodate what you are praying for?

I will never forget the first time I bought a car on my own. I was in college, and I was so excited about that vehicle—it was a good car, it was exactly the color I wanted, and it was fast. However, I didn't have a lot of experience taking care of cars. Once, when I took the vehicle to be serviced, the technician asked me when I had last taken it for an oil change. I told him it had been a year. He started to laugh hysterically!

The truth was, I wasn't ready to own a car of that caliber. Similarly, many Christians all over the world are asking God for things they don't have the capacity to receive. What will you do after you receive what you have prayed for? Are you prepared for that spouse? Are you ready for that promotion? Have you developed the life of prayer and devotion necessary to sustain your dream ministry or next assignment?

It is clear that one of the keys to supernatural breakthrough is preparation. The Shunammite woman recognized that Elisha was a man of God, so she extended special hospitality to him. By creating space for the prophet, she was actually making room for a miracle. We must take notes from the life of this great woman of faith and get into position ourselves to receive the things we are believing God for. The Shunammite woman had no idea she would become a mother after years of barrenness, simply by being wise enough to make room for one who was doing God's work. But she opened her life to God's blessings. (See 2 Kings 4:14–17.)

Change your thinking! Change your attitude! Take on a different disposition. Remember, the attitude of expectancy is the breeding ground for miracles. Don't wait until you see the manifestation. Make room now!

Prayer of Divine Protection

Father, You are the Lord of the breakthrough, and I know that You have met every need in my life. By faith, I receive Your miraculous provision and all the blessings You have graciously prepared for Your children. I position myself to receive the manifestation of Your promises in my life. I declare that my thoughts, words, and actions will align with heaven's agenda. I recognize that now is the time of my supernatural visitation. In Jesus' name, amen!

Doubt

In the multitude of my thoughts within me Your comforts delight my soul. (Psalm 94:19)

And Jesus answering said to them, Have faith in God. For verily I say to you, That whosoever shall say to this mountain, Be you removed, and be you cast into the sea; and shall not doubt in his heart, but shall believe that those things which he says shall come to pass; he shall have whatsoever he says. (Mark 11:22–23)

All things are possible to him that believes. (Mark 9:23)

Be strong and of a good courage; be not afraid, neither be you dismayed: for the LORD your God is with you wherever you go. (Joshua 1:9)

Whatsoever you shall ask in prayer, believing, you shall receive. (Matthew 21:22)

Faith is the substance of things hoped for, the evidence of things not seen. (Hebrews 11:1)

Beloved, if our heart condemn us not, then have we confidence toward God. And whatsoever we ask, we receive of Him, because we keep His commandments, and do those things that are pleasing in His sight. (1 John 3:21–22)

Trouble

God is our refuge and strength, a very present help in trouble. (Psalm 46:1)

The salvation of the righteous is of the LORD: He is their strength in the time of trouble. And the LORD shall help them, and deliver them: He shall deliver them from the wicked, and save them, because they trust in him.

(Psalm 37:39–40)

Many are the afflictions of the righteous: but the LORD delivers him out of them all. (Psalm 34:19)

These things I have spoken to you, that in Me you might have peace. In the world you shall have tribulation: but be of good cheer; I have overcome the world. (John 16:33)

Because he has set his love upon Me, therefore will I deliver him: I will set him on high, because he has known My name. He shall call upon Me, and I will answer him: I will be with him in trouble; I will deliver him, and honor him.

(Psalm 91:14–15)

When you pass through the waters, I will be with you; and through the rivers, they shall not overflow you: when you walk through the fire, you shall not be burned; neither shall the flame kindle upon you. For I am the LORD your God, the Holy One of Israel, your Savior.   (Isaiah 43:2–3)

Temptation

For we have not a high priest which cannot be touched with the feeling of our infirmities; but was in all points tempted like as we are, yet without sin. Let us therefore come boldly to the throne of grace, that we may obtain mercy, and find grace to help in time of need.   (Hebrews 4:15–16)

There has no temptation taken you but such as is common to man: but God is faithful, who will not suffer you to be tempted above that you are able; but will with the temptation also make a way to escape, that you may be able to bear it.

(1 Corinthians 10:13)

[God] delivered just Lot, vexed with the filthy conversation of the wicked...the Lord knows how to deliver the godly out of temptations, and to reserve the unjust unto the day of judgment to be punished.   (2 Peter 2:7–9)

Abstain from all appearance of evil. And the very God of peace sanctify you wholly; and I pray God your whole spirit and soul and body be preserved blameless to the coming of our Lord Jesus Christ. Faithful is He that calls you, who also will do it.   (1 Thessalonians 5:22–24)

Blessed is the man that endures temptation: for when he is tried, he shall receive the crown of life, which the Lord has promised to them that love Him.   (James 1:12)

Satanic Attack

Wherefore take to you the whole armor of God, that you may be able to withstand in the evil day, and having done all, to stand. (Ephesians 6:13)

Submit yourselves therefore to God. Resist the devil, and he will flee from you. (James 4:7)

We know that whosoever is born of God sins not; but he that is begotten of God keeps himself, and that wicked one touches him not. (1 John 5:18)

Our Lord Jesus Christ...gave Himself for our sins, that He might deliver us from this present evil world, according to the will of God and our Father. (Galatians 1:3–4)

The God of peace shall bruise Satan under your feet shortly. The grace of our Lord Jesus Christ be with you.

(Romans 16:20)

I pray not that You should take them out of the world, but that You should keep them from the evil. They are not of the world, even as I am not of the world.

(John 17:15–16)

We know that we are of God, and the whole world lies in wickedness. (1 John 5:19)

Trial

Blessed is the man that endures temptation: for when he is tried, he shall receive the crown of life, which the Lord has promised to them that love Him. (James 1:12)

We glory in tribulations also: knowing that tribulation works patience. (Romans 5:3)

My brethren, count it all joy when you fall into divers temptations; knowing this, that the trying of your faith works patience. But let patience have her perfect work, that you may be perfect and entire, wanting nothing. (James 1:2–4)

[You] are kept by the power of God through faith to salvation ready to be revealed in the last time. Wherein you greatly rejoice, though now for a season, if need be, you are in heaviness through manifold temptations: that the trial of your faith, being much more precious than of gold that perishes, though it be tried with fire, might be found to praise and honor and glory at the appearing of Jesus Christ.

(1 Peter 1:5–7)

Sickness

Blessed is he that considers the poor.... The LORD will strengthen him upon the bed of languishing.

(Psalm 41:1, 3)

And the LORD will take away from you all sickness, and will put none of the evil diseases of Egypt, which you know, upon you. (Deuteronomy 7:15)

I will take sickness away from the midst of you.

(Exodus 23:25)

These signs shall follow them that believe...they shall lay hands on the sick, and they shall recover.

(Mark 16:17–18)

Is any sick among you? let him call for the elders of the church; and let them pray over him, anointing him with oil in the name of the Lord: And the prayer of faith shall save the sick, and the Lord shall raise him up.

(James 5:14–15)

Many as touched were made perfectly whole.

(Matthew 14:36)

He cast out the spirits with His word, and healed all that were sick: That it might be fulfilled which was spoken by Isaiah the prophet, saying, Himself took our infirmities, and bore our sicknesses. (Matthew 8:16–17)

Death

It is appointed to men once to die. (Hebrews 9:27)

Yea, though I walk through the valley of the shadow of death, I will fear no evil: for You are with me; Your rod and Your staff they comfort me. (Psalm 23:4)

O death, where is your sting? O grave, where is your victory? The sting of death is sin; and the strength of sin is the law. But thanks be to God, which gives us the victory through our Lord Jesus Christ. (1 Corinthians 15:55–57)

For this corruptible must put on incorruption, and this mortal must put on immortality. So when this corruptible shall have put on incorruption, and this mortal shall have put on immortality, then shall be brought to pass the saying that is written, Death is swallowed up in victory.

(1 Corinthians 15:53–54)

We are confident, I say, and willing rather to be absent from the body, and to be present with the Lord. Wherefore we labor, that, whether present or absent, we may be accepted of him. (2 Corinthians 5:8–9)

In My Father's house are many mansions: if it were not so, I would have told you. I go to prepare a place for you. And if I go and prepare a place for you, I will come again, and receive you to Myself; that where I am, there you may be also.
(John 14:2–3)

I am persuaded, that neither death, nor life, nor angels, nor principalities, nor powers, nor things present, nor things to come...shall be able to separate us from the love of God, which is in Christ Jesus our Lord.
(Romans 8:38–39)

Sorrow

Blessed are they that mourn: for they shall be comforted.
(Matthew 5:4)

You now therefore have sorrow: but I will see you again, and your heart shall rejoice, and your joy no man takes from you. (John 16:22)

They that sow in tears shall reap in joy. He that goes forth and weeps, bearing precious seed, shall doubtless come again with rejoicing, bringing his sheaves with him.
(Psalm 126:5–6)

The LORD has comforted His people, and will have mercy upon His afflicted. (Isaiah 49:13)

The redeemed of the LORD shall return, and come with singing to Zion; and everlasting joy shall be upon their head: they shall obtain gladness and joy; and sorrow and mourning shall flee away. (Isaiah 51:11)

Then shall the virgin rejoice in the dance, both young men and old together: for I will turn their mourning into joy, and will comfort them, and make them rejoice from their sorrow. (Jeremiah 31:13)

Weeping may endure for a night, but joy comes in the morning. (Psalm 30:5)

And God shall wipe away all tears from their eyes; and there shall be no more death, neither sorrow, nor crying, neither shall there be any more pain: for the former things are passed away. (Revelation 21:4)

Backsliding

A voice was heard upon the high places, weeping and supplications of the children of Israel: for they have perverted their way, and they have forgotten the LORD their God. Return, you backsliding children, and I will heal your backslidings.

(Jeremiah 3:21–22)

Come now, and let us reason together, says the LORD: though your sins be as scarlet, they shall be as white as snow; though they be red like crimson, they shall be as wool.

(Isaiah 1:18)

Your ears shall hear a word behind you, saying, This is the way, walk you in it. (Isaiah 30:21)

I have blotted out, as a thick cloud, your transgressions, and, as a cloud, your sins: return to Me; for I have redeemed you. (Isaiah 44:22)

All we like sheep have gone astray; we have turned every one to his own way; and the Lord has laid on Him the iniquity of us all. (Isaiah 53:6)

I have seen his ways, and will heal him: I will lead him also, and restore comforts to him…. Peace, peace to him that is far off, and to him that is near, says the Lord; and I will heal him. (Isaiah 57:18–19)

My little children, these things write I to you, that you sin not. And if any man sin, we have an advocate with the Father, Jesus Christ the righteous. (1 John 2:1)

Personal Attack

If God be for us, who can be against us? (Romans 8:31)

The salvation of the righteous is of the Lord….. The Lord shall deliver them from the wicked, and save them, because they trust in him. (Psalm 37:39–40)

The Lord is my light and my salvation; whom shall I fear? the Lord is the strength of my life; of whom shall I be afraid? When the wicked, even my enemies and my foes, came upon me to eat up my flesh, they stumbled and fell. (Psalm 27:1–2)

Let all those that put their trust in You rejoice: let them ever shout for joy, because You defend them. (Psalm 5:11)

Be courteous: not rendering evil for evil, or railing for railing: but contrariwise blessing; knowing that you are thereunto called, that you should inherit a blessing.

(1 Peter 3:8–9)

They shall fight against you, but they shall not prevail against you: for I am with you to save you and to deliver you, says the LORD. And I will deliver you out of the hand of the wicked, and I will redeem you out of the hand of the terrible.   (Jeremiah 15:20–21)

Fear you not, stand still, and see the salvation of the LORD, which He will show to you to day.... The LORD shall fight for you, and you shall hold your peace.

(Exodus 14:13–14)

Persecution

Blessed are they which are persecuted for righteousness' sake: for theirs is the kingdom of heaven.   (Matthew 5:10)

Blessed are you, when men shall revile you, and persecute you, and shall say all manner of evil against you falsely, for My sake. Rejoice, and be exceeding glad: for great is your reward in heaven: for so persecuted they the prophets which were before you.   (Matthew 5:11–12)

Love your enemies, bless them that curse you, do good to them that hate you, and pray for them which spitefully use you, and persecute you; that you may be the children of your Father which is in heaven.   (Matthew 5:44–45)

They shall lay their hands on you, and persecute you…. Settle it therefore in your hearts, not to meditate before what you shall answer: for I will give you a mouth and wisdom, which all your adversaries shall not be able to gainsay nor resist. (Luke 21:12, 14–15)

You shall be hated of all men for My name's sake. But there shall not a hair of your head perish. In your patience possess you your souls. (Luke 21:17–19)

Fear none of those things which you shall suffer: behold, the devil shall cast some of you into prison, that you may be tried…be you faithful to death, and I will give you a crown of life. (Revelation 2:10)

It is a faithful saying: For if we be dead with Him, we shall also live with Him: if we suffer, we shall also reign with Him. (2 Timothy 2:11–12)

We are troubled on every side, yet not distressed; we are perplexed, but not in despair; persecuted, but not forsaken; cast down, but not destroyed. (2 Corinthians 4:8–9)

If we believe not, yet He abides faithful: He cannot deny Himself. (2 Timothy 2:13)

About the Author

Dr. Kynan T. Bridges is the senior pastor of Grace & Peace Global Fellowship in Tampa, Florida. With a profound revelation of the Word of God and a dynamic teaching ministry, Dr. Bridges has revolutionized the lives of many in the body of Christ. Through his practical approach to applying the deep truths of the Word of God, he reveals the authority and identity of the new covenant believer.

God has placed on Dr. Bridges a particular anointing for understanding and teaching the Scriptures, along with the gifts of prophecy and healing. Dr. Bridges and his wife, Gloria, through an apostolic anointing, are committed to equipping the body of Christ to live in the supernatural every day and to fulfill the Great Commission. It is the desire of Dr. Bridges to see the nations transformed by the unconditional love of God.

A highly sought speaker and published author of a number of books, his previous books with Whitaker House include *School of the Miraculous, Invading the Heavens,*

Unmasking the Accuser, The Power of Prophetic Prayer, and *Kingdom Authority.* Dr. Bridges is a committed husband, a mentor, and a father of five beautiful chiidren: Ella, Naomi, Isaac, Israel, and Anna.